# Five Holidays

by Holly Harper

illustrated by Lesley Danson

OXFORD
UNIVERSITY PRESS
AUSTRALIA & NEW ZEALAND

The Chen family were trying to choose a holiday.

"I love animals," said Grandfather. "We could go on a nature watching trip."

"No!" said Dad. "Let's go to a place with yummy food. We can try some new dishes."

"I don't like cooking," said Ivy. "I want to go and listen to some music. I want to dance."

"That sounds too loud!" said Mum.
"I just want some peace and quiet."

"I want an adventure," said Grandmother.
"What about rock climbing or
bike racing?"

The Chens started to argue. They each wanted *their* holiday. Nobody wanted to budge.

Dylan knew they would never agree.

"What do you think, Dylan?" Grandfather finally asked. "Which holiday should we go on?"

"I don't know," Dylan said. "I like the sound of all of them."

"Well, we can't go on five holidays," said Mum. "We only have a few days."

"Maybe we *can* have five holidays," said Dylan. "What if we stayed right here?"

"A holiday at home?" said Grandmother. "That's no fun."

"Please, let's try it," said Dylan. "I'll design the Chen's holiday at home!"

On Monday, the Chens went on a nature watching trip ... in their garden.

Grandfather told them the names of the birds they saw.

"Look!" he said. "A blue wren."

On Tuesday, the Chens went to a place with yummy food ... their kitchen. Dad made fried chicken in breadcrumbs.

"This is so tasty!" said Dylan.

"I don't like cooking, but I *do* like eating," said Ivy.

The next day they listened to music and danced.

They all sang along. Mum's voice was the loudest!

On Thursday ... they relaxed.

They lounged around. Mum and Grandmother put face packs on.

"This will fix our wrinkles," said Mum.

"I like my wrinkles," said Grandmother.

On Friday, they had a bicycle race near their house.

Nobody could catch up with Grandmother!
They cheered when she won.

"That was the best holiday ever!" said Ivy. "We all got what we wanted."

Mum turned to Dylan. "What about you, Dylan? What would you like to do?"

Dylan knew what he wanted to do for his holiday.

"Let's watch something on TV," he said.

"It's Dylan's turn to pick," said Dad.

"I know! Let's watch them all," said Dylan.